CAPTURED
SCIENCE
HISTORY

DOUBLE HELIX

HOW AN IMAGE SPARKED THE DISCOVERY OF THE SECRET OF LIFE

by Danielle Smith-Llera

Content Adviser: Brett Barker, PhD
Associate Professor of History
University of Wisconsin—Marathon County

COMPASS POINT BOOKS
a capstone imprint

Compass Point Books are published by Capstone,
1710 Roe Crest Drive, North Mankato, Minnesota 56003
www.mycapstone.com

Editor: Catherine Neitge
Designers: Tracy Davies McCabe and Catherine Neitge
Media Researcher: Svetlana Zhurkin
Library Consultant: Kathleen Baxter
Production Specialist: Laura Manthe

Image Credits
Alamy: National Geographic Creative, 21; Dreamstime: Andrey Salamchev, 19, 56;
From the Ava Helen and Linus Pauling Papers, OSU Libraries Special Collections
& Archives Research Center, 11, 35, 57; Getty Images: SSPL/Bletchley Park Trust,
27, The *LIFE* Images Collection/Mark Kauffman, 49, The *LIFE* Picture Collection/
Fritz Goro, 47, 58 (top), UIG/Universal History Archive, 5, 9, 13, ullstein bild/
ADN-Bildarchiv, 41; Newscom: akg-images, 31, 44, Heritage Image/*Jewish Chronicle*,
33, Photoshot/UPPA, 12, World History Archive, 7; Science Source: 24, 29, 36, 37,
A. Barrington Brown, 17, 39, James King-Holmes, 43, 51, 58 (bottom), Sam Ogden,
53, Wellcome Images, 22; Shutterstock: angellodeco, 59 (bottom), Designua, 45,
GSerban, 59 (top), nobeastsofierce, cover, 15, Tony Baggett, 6, vitstudio, 55

Library of Congress Cataloging-in-Publication Data

Names: Smith-Llera, Danielle, 1971¬– author.
Title: Double helix: how an image sparked the discovery of the secret of life / by
Danielle Smith-Llera.
Description: North Mankato, Minnesota : Compass Point Books, a Capstone imprint,
[2018] | Series: Captured science history | Audience: Age 10-12. | Audience: Grade 4
to 6. | Includes bibliographical references and index.
Identifiers: LCCN 2017010278| ISBN 9780756556426 (library binding) | ISBN
9780756556464 (paperback) | ISBN 9780756556501 (ebook pdf)
Subjects: LCSH: DNA—Juvenile literature. | DNA—Research—History—Juvenile
literature.
Classification: LCC QP624.S62 2018 | DDC 572.8/6—dc23
LC record available at https://lccn.loc.gov/2017010278

Printed in the United States of America.
010374F17

TABLEOFCONTENTS

Chapter One

GLIMPSE OF A PHOTO

James Watson carried a document with him on the 50-mile (80-kilometer) train trip from Cavendish Laboratory in Cambridge, England, to London. The paper had already traveled more than 5,000 miles (8,047 km) from California before arriving in his hands that late January day in 1953. He could not wait to share the news it held.

The American biologist hurried along the wide courtyard of King's College in London where a German bomb had destroyed underground labs just over a decade earlier. World War II had demanded the skills of many scientists, including those of Maurice Wilkins, the friend he was heading to see in the King's College physics labs.

Wilkins had worked to improve radar, then traveled to Berkeley, California, to help develop the first nuclear weapons. But by the end of the war, he felt "very disgusted with the dropping of two bombs on civilian centers in Japan" and returned to England and to King's College to study something new.

Inside the physics labs, Wilkins peered into cells, deep inside the nucleus, to a molecule called deoxyribonucleic acid—DNA for short. No one fully understood the shape or construction of the molecule. Many other scientists were more interested

in studying the cell's proteins. After all, they are complex and direct nearly every task in the human body. Yet some scientists, including Wilkins, hoped that finding the simple structure of the DNA molecule would help answer a great mystery of life: How do organisms live, grow, develop, and survive, generation after generation?

Watson thought the answer might lie in DNA. Questions about the mysterious molecule had brought

King George IV and the Duke of Wellington founded King's College London in 1829. It is part of the University of London.

him across the Atlantic Ocean to labs in Europe three years earlier. It was well known that DNA was composed of a few basic parts: phosphate and sugar molecules that were linked to form chains. Scientists also knew that DNA contained four types of nitrogen-based molecules, called bases: adenine, cytosine, guanine, and thymine. But how did these simple building blocks all fit together?

Watson burst into King's physics labs, eager to share a new scientific paper written by Linus Pauling of the California Institute of Technology. It described

how these simple parts could build a DNA molecule. Twenty-four-year old Watson admired Pauling, the 51-year-old chemist who had discovered that protein molecules could take the shape of a coil, called an alpha helix. In a 1950 lecture, Pauling had presented his model of the single staircase-like structure and received worldwide praise. "There was no one like Linus in all the world," Watson once wrote. "The combination of his prodigious mind and infectious grin was unbeatable."

But the famed chemist had blundered with DNA,

and Watson knew it. Pauling's mistake was contained in a diagram in the paper Watson clutched. Pauling imagined a triple helix of phosphate and sugar chains twisting around each other with the nitrogen bases attached and pointing outward, like leaves on a tree branch. Watson knew this theory was wrong because he had made an inaccurate triple helix model himself a year earlier.

On his way to find Wilkins, Watson stopped by the office of another scientist, Rosalind Franklin. X-ray photographs and books were spread across her desk. She was also deep into studying DNA's structure, but she was not interested in Pauling's diagram. She distrusted the celebrated scientist's method. He had discovered the alpha helix structure in just a few hours, by drawing on paper while sick in bed. Franklin believed sketches or models could only come after meticulously collecting data. She took careful measurements and made calculations based on her X-ray photographs of the DNA molecule. Numbers and notes filled her notebooks, not drawings.

Wilkins welcomed his friend Watson into his office. He was glad for an opportunity to grumble about Franklin. Though Wilkins and Franklin both studied DNA, they competed rather than worked together. The lab's director, John Randall, had even given them separate workspaces and divided the DNA research so they could work independently.

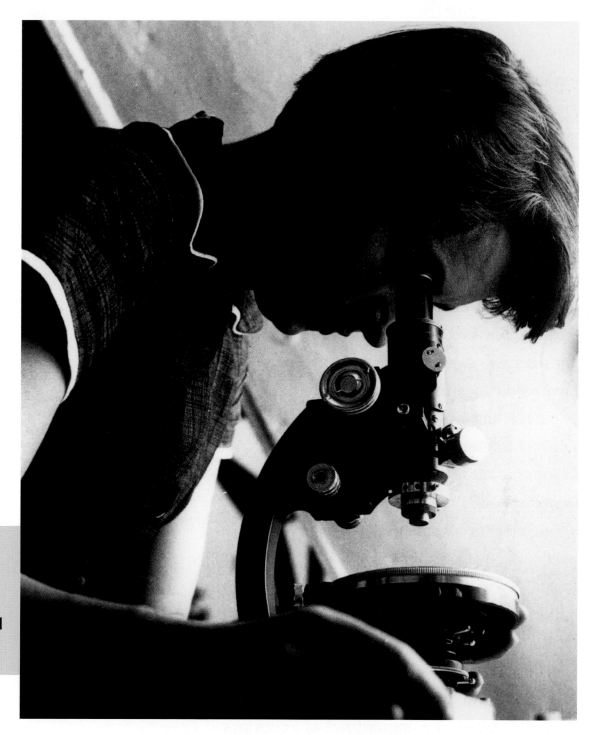

Women, including scientist Rosalind Franklin, were not always welcomed to the male-dominated collegiate world.

Franklin enjoyed working alone, but she also found King's College old-fashioned and unwelcoming. Scientists gathered in a men-only commons room for lunch and discussion. She wrote to a friend in Paris that, at King's, there was "nobody with whom I particularly want to discuss anything, scientific or otherwise."

Franklin refused to discuss anything scientific with Watson during his trip to the King's labs. Yet, without knowing it, she would help him and his Cambridge colleague Francis Crick make history. Out of a drawer in his office, Wilkins pulled an X-ray photograph made in the lab by Franklin and her assistant, Raymond Gosling. She had labeled it "Photo 51." Without asking her permission—and in a move that many scientists have said is unethical—Wilkins showed it to Watson.

To the untrained eye, the photograph was simply a grainy black and white image of dark marks scattered in roughly the shape of an "X." But to someone skilled in crystallography—the science of determining the arrangement of atoms in crystals—it was a clear portrait of a DNA fiber taken with X-rays. John Bernal, an early developer of the X-ray photography technique, praised Franklin for the "extreme clarity and perfection in everything she undertook. Her photographs are among the most beautiful X-ray photographs of any substance ever taken."

Wilkins knew the importance of Franklin's Photo 51. The X shape confirmed his guess of DNA's structure. "I had this photograph, and there was a helix right on the picture. You couldn't miss it," he

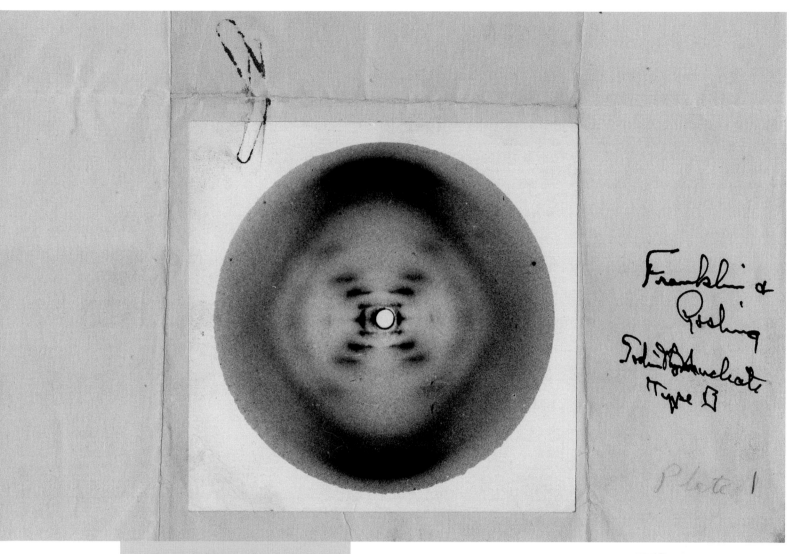

Linus Pauling received a copy of Photo 51, taken by Rosalind Franklin. The name of her graduate assistant, Raymond Gosling, also appears on the note.

later said. Watson saw it too. "The instant I saw the picture my mouth fell open and my pulse started to race," he remembered.

While riding the train back to Cambridge, Watson drew what he remembered of Photo 51 in the margin of a newspaper. Helices curved around each other like spiral staircases. He did not want to forget what he had seen before he could share it with his lab mate, Francis Crick. Unlike Wilkins and Franklin, he and Crick were friendly and shared ideas. The simplicity of the image he had seen excited him. When he got back to the lab, he waited for Crick. "Francis did not get halfway through the door before I let loose that the answer to everything was in our hands," Watson said later.

But seeing the drawing based on Franklin's superb photograph also worried Watson. He supposed that if Pauling "put one of his assistants to taking DNA photographs" they might get one as clear as Photo 51 and "in a week at most, Linus would have the structure."

Watson and Crick raced to be first in solving the mystery of DNA's structure. They had no time for data collection. They would build a model in three dimensions. Too impatient to wait for the lab machine shop to cut metal into model-making pieces to get started, they used cardboard cutouts.

Franklin's Photo 51 still left important questions unanswered. It showed DNA was a helix, but not how many chains twirled around each other like stripes on a candy stick. It did not show whether the nitrogen bases fit inside the chains like ladder rungs or sprouted outward. For several weeks the scientists arranged and rearranged the pieces in their lab.

On the morning of February 28, 1953, Watson made a new arrangement of the pieces. They fitted together in an elegant form that swooped in two

Francis Crick became a molecular biologist after first studying physics.

ROSALIND FRANKLIN: THE WOMAN BEHIND PHOTO 51

Rosalind Franklin

When 15-year-old Rosalind Franklin decided to become a scientist in the 1930s, her father worried. Most scientists at the time were men. The British Royal Society, which promotes scientific research, was established in 1662 but did not admit a female scientist until 1945.

Franklin studied chemistry at Cambridge University and went on to receive a PhD. "Cambridge really did for Rosalind everything that a good university should. It gave her a profession, a philosophy of life," said her biographer, Brenda Maddox. "She emerged a mature, socially and politically aware individual, and she was ready to become a working scientist." She soon won admiration for her early work in a Paris lab in the 1940s. She pioneered the use of X-ray photography to study the structure of coal. A colleague wrote, "I considered her a genius, and I don't use that word lightly."

In 1951 she began work at King's College in London using her X-ray techniques to study DNA. James Watson and Francis Crick admitted in 1954 that their solution to the DNA structure "would have been most unlikely, if not impossible" without Franklin's X-ray data. Still, they did not treat her as an equal. "I'm afraid we always used to adopt—let's say, a patronizing attitude towards her," Crick later said.

After leaving King's College, Franklin became well known for her work on the structure of viruses, including the polio virus. Her work was cut short by her death from ovarian cancer in 1958, when she was just 37 years old. Years of exposure to X-rays was likely the cause.

Her list of admirers has only grown in the decades since. In his 1982 Nobel Prize acceptance speech, Aaron Klug, a friend and collaborator, spoke of her inspiring "example of tackling large and difficult problems."

A plaque marks where she lived and worked in London. And every year the British Royal Society presents the Rosalind Franklin Award to support women working in science, technology, engineering, and math.

spiral staircases curving around each other for 6 feet (1.8 meters). Crick walked in and "it was quite a moment," Watson later remembered. "We felt sure that this was it. Anything that simple, that elegant, just had to be right." Besides its beauty, Crick also recognized the logic of the structure—the two ladders could unzip to allow the DNA molecule to copy itself countless times.

The double-helix structure answered questions scientists had puzzled over for centuries. Watson was very pleased that his and Crick's names "would be associated with the double helix as Pauling's was with the alpha helix." In fact, the simple and symmetrical structure would find admirers well beyond the science community. Over the following decades it became so familiar that designers and artists worked it into artwork, clothing, and business logos.

"We're very famous because DNA is very famous," Watson said of himself and Crick in 2003. In the decades since they built the first accurate model, the world has found that what led to it is complex. Without the work of Franklin—and some luck—Watson and Crick might not have been the ones to introduce the double helix to the world after all.

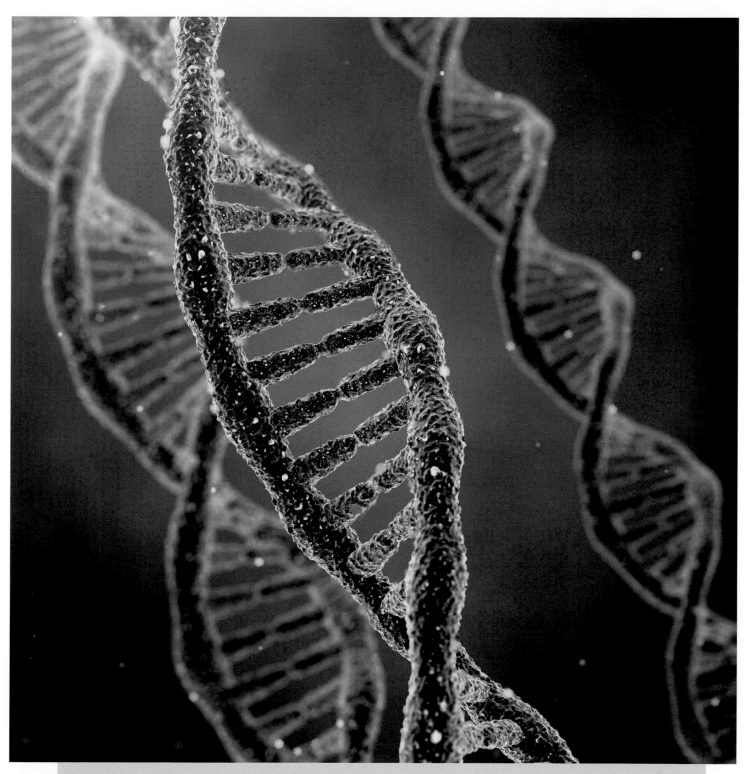

Hereditary information is stored as a code in DNA, deoxyribonucleic acid.

ChapterTwo
LONG CHAIN OF DISCOVERIES

Photographer Antony Barrington Brown visited Cavendish Laboratory in May 1953 on assignment for *Time* magazine. He photographed Francis Crick and James Watson posing with their DNA model. But the magazine missed the significance of the discovery. It did not publish a photograph or even an article at the time. In fact, several discoveries that helped make Crick and Watson's discovery possible were also overlooked at first. Maybe their significance was not entirely clear until the morning all the puzzle pieces came together in the Cavendish Laboratory.

People have realized for centuries that human beings share traits with their parents and ancestors. But they used to wonder how the similarities travel across generations. It was once believed that only fathers passed traits on to their children. In the fourth century BCE, the Greek philosopher Aristotle proposed a more complex theory. He suggested that children received hereditary information, like a message, from parents and generations of ancestors.

It would be 2,000 years before people began examining this "message" scientifically. They tried to understand the physical laws that control the natural world. They used microscopes, telescopes, and mathematics to collect data and test their theories.

The iconic photo of James Watson (left), Francis Crick, and their DNA model was not published for 15 years after it was taken in 1953.

Astronomer Galileo, mathematician Isaac Newton, and other scientists discovered that laws of physics control how objects move on Earth and how planets move in space.

Two famous scientists in the 19th century helped to discover how hereditary traits travel across generations. In search of an explanation, the English naturalist Charles Darwin took a five-year voyage around the world. Gregor Mendel, a monk in what is now the Czech Republic, studied thousands of pea plants in his monastery garden for eight years. Both took careful notes and developed theories about what they had observed.

Darwin caused a great stir with a new theory that was published in 1859. He argued that only traits that helped an animal species to survive, such as speed or coloring, were passed down over generations. This idea, coupled with other theories, would later be called the theory of evolution.

But Darwin did not understand exactly how traits were passed from parents to offspring. Like many scientists at the time, he believed that each parent had bits of information flowing through its blood, collected from their organs and tissues. He thought this information was blended together when offspring were produced.

Mendel's pea plants proved that Darwin was wrong about heredity. Mendel crossbred plants by transferring pollen between plants with a paintbrush. He examined the offspring to see how characteristics such as flower color and stem height moved across generations. If traits blended together, as Darwin believed, then a tall plant and short plant would always produce a medium-sized plant. But Mendel's experiments showed that tall and short plants produced both tall and short plants in succeeding generations—the traits disappearing and reappearing unchanged.

Mendel concluded that traits traveled as unchanged units—never blended, only shuffled and reshuffled into new arrangements. Some traits, called dominant traits, had more influence than others and appeared more often. Less influential traits, called recessive traits, would continue to appear but less often in following generations. Each generation of offspring inherits a collection of these pieces of hereditary information. Today they are called genes.

Mendel published his work in 1866, but his discovery went unnoticed for decades. In 1900 English biologist William Bateson came upon Mendel's work and instantly felt "in the presence of a new principle of the highest importance." He traveled and spread the news of Mendel's discovery. Experiments by other scientists at the time confirmed that his theory was at work not only in plants and animals, but also in humans.

Bateson helped usher in a new field of science. The study of heredity came to be known as genetics, a term related to the Greek word *genno*, which means "to give birth." Geneticists focused on such basic questions as these: What is a gene? Where is it and how does it work?

Mendel had used only the naked eye to collect data. But in the 1880s scientists peered through microscopes at the nuclei of cells dividing. They watched as many long threads coiled together into X-shapes passed between the cells. Because the threads absorbed colored dyes easily, they were first called chromatin, which meant stainable material. The name was changed to chromosomes in 1888.

German biologist Theodor Boveri and American geneticist Walter Sutton concluded in 1903 that chromosomes contain all the hereditary information needed for an organism to grow and function.

Studying marine life in separate labs, they found that embryos only developed normally if the full number of chromosomes were present.

American biologist Thomas Hunt Morgan set out to see for himself how heredity worked. In a lab he bred generations of fruit flies to see how dominant and recessive traits for eye color and wing shape appeared across generations. Morgan's findings, collected over nearly two decades, closely reflected

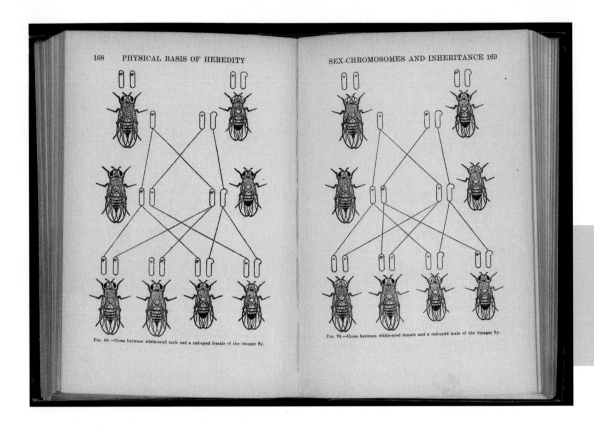

Fig. 69.—Cross between white-eyed male and a red-eyed female of the vinegar fly.

Fig. 70.—Cross between white-eyed female and a red-eyed male of the vinegar fly.

Thomas Hunt Morgan's book *The Physical Basis of Heredity* was published in 1919.

Mendel's data. Morgan won the 1933 Nobel Prize in Physiology or Medicine because he did more than confirm Mendel's finding. He figured out how genes fit into chromosomes. He noticed that traits moved between generations in groups. For example, dark-colored flies always had a certain shape of wing. He realized that genes for these traits must be close together on the same chromosome, lined up like "beads on a string."

But what were these strings of genes made of? In 1869 a Swiss biologist named Friedrich Miescher was the first to isolate the substance. He collected white blood cells from pus-filled hospital bandages. He extracted the nuclei and used special solutions to wash away all known materials such as proteins, carbohydrates, and fats. Miescher was left with a mysterious gray, sticky substance. It would be more than 50 years before discovery of the new substance drew much attention. It would be called nucleic acid, and then, in the 1950s, DNA, an abbreviation for deoxyribonucleic acid.

By the 1920s scientists had identified the chemicals in nucleic acid—a sugar molecule called deoxyribose, phosphates, and nitrogen bases. They knew that the structures of DNA molecules were long chains. But how they fit together was still a puzzle.

Many scientists were not curious about the DNA molecule. Because it had just three components, one scientist called it "comically plain." It seemed much more likely that genes were made of proteins found in chromosomes. After all, proteins come in many complex shapes. They instruct cells everywhere in the body how to function. Why could they not carry detailed genetic instructions from one generation to the next?

To solve this problem, scientists turned away from plants and animals, even from the tiny fruit fly, to the microscopic world of bacteria. In 1928 British scientist Frederick Griffith proved that bacteria have an astonishing ability—they can share genetic information by simply being in contact with each other. He proved that when mixed together, a deadly

THE POWER OF A SIMPLE MOLECULE

Oswald Avery was one of the first molecular biologists.

Oswald Avery has been called a "quiet revolutionary." He and other researchers at the Rockefeller Institute in New York City had worked for nearly a decade in the 1930s and 1940s to discover the chemistry of the gene. Finally Avery dissolved away bacteria's substances, such as proteins and sugars, one at a time. When only DNA remained, he discovered that the bacteria could still share genetic information when it reproduced. He had proved beyond doubt that DNA was the carrier of heredity.

Yet Avery's work was not immediately considered groundbreaking or even accurate. Many scientists still believed that a tiny amount of protein inside DNA molecules carry genetic information, not the deoxyribose nucleic acid itself. Avery died in 1955, without having received a Nobel Prize.

Even scientists who believed that genes are made of DNA overlooked Avery. None of the three papers on DNA published by James Watson, Francis Crick, Maurice Wilkins, and Rosalind Franklin in 1953 mentioned Avery's work. But his discovery inspired biochemist Erwin Chargaff to make his own discoveries about DNA's chemicals, work that was essential to Watson and Crick when finishing their model of DNA's structure. Today Avery is admired for providing the foundation of modern DNA research and being part of a "molecular revolution in genetics."

strain of pneumococcal bacteria can make a harmless strain deadly.

But this discovery did not inspire debate or even interest among his fellow scientists until nearly two decades later. A Canadian-born physician and researcher, Oswald Avery took Griffith's experiment further. He wanted to know what chemical carried the genetic information between bacteria. Was it a protein or something else? In 1944 Avery published a startling, and unpopular, discovery—genes were not made of proteins after all, but of DNA. By experimenting with the same deadly and harmless strains as Griffith, he had isolated the pale, stringy substance that allowed deadly bacteria to transform harmless bacteria. It was DNA, the molecule dismissed as "boring" by many scientists.

By the 1950s many experiments had shown that genes are made of DNA. Scientists turned to DNA with new interest and to Avery's work with admiration. An Austro-Hungarian biochemist, Erwin Chargaff, said Avery "gave us the first text of a new language, or rather he showed us where to look for it."

But DNA molecules are much too small to study with a microscope. Scientists such as Watson, Crick, Franklin, and Wilkins would have to use X-rays, math, imagination, and common sense to learn DNA's structure. Knowing the structure would reveal how the molecule works, carrying instructions to cells across generations.

ChapterThree
RACING TO THE PRIZE

"We were lucky with DNA," Francis Crick recalled, years after his famous discovery. One of many bits of luck he and James Watson enjoyed came in the form of a small book, easily read in a few hours. Written by Austrian physicist Erwin Schrödinger and published in 1944, it made many scientists who were on well-worn career paths try a new direction. Its title was simply *What Is Life?* Schrödinger argued that understanding the gene was the answer. He believed that DNA contained an "architect's plan" for a living organism.

The book changed the course of Watson's life when he read it as a 17-year-old. "In that little gem," he later recalled, "Schrödinger said the essence of life was the gene. Up until then, I was interested in birds. But then I thought, well, if the gene is the essence of life, I want to know more about it." By age 22, when most students are just completing their bachelor's degrees, Watson had earned a PhD in zoology. He left the United States for Europe in 1950 with the dream of understanding DNA.

Schrödinger also inspired scientists to look beyond the limits of their scientific fields. New Zealand-born Maurice Wilkins was trained in physics, but he explored biology too. Also a trained

physicist, Crick taught himself biology and chemistry in his spare time. Understanding DNA's purpose and structure depended on knowledge collected by many kinds of scientists.

Besides a small book, an epic war drove scientists to understand how DNA carried messages. World War II disrupted the academic lives of scientists, but it also brought many kinds of scientists together. They shared ideas. Mathematicians were experimenting with cracking Nazi Germany's secret coded messages that were carried by radio waves. They also began writing simple code to program early computers. Scientists wondered whether DNA's genetic information could also be in the form of a simple code.

Another admirer of Schrödinger realized the logic of DNA's simple code in the late 1940s. Biochemist Erwin Chargaff noticed a curious pattern in DNA's nitrogen bases—in every species he tested, adenine and thymine always appeared in the same amounts. Cytosine and guanine appeared in the same amounts too. This discovery would allow Watson and Crick to solve the puzzle of DNA structure.

Luck nudged Watson toward his goal soon after he arrived in Europe. Almost two years before showing Watson Photo 51, Wilkins had unveiled another unforgettable X-ray photograph. Watson was in the audience when Wilkins presented a blurry X-ray photograph at a lecture in Naples, Italy, in April 1951. It was a low-quality image from his early efforts in crystallography, exposing DNA fibers to X-rays for up to 60 hours. Yet Watson was captivated. "The fact that I was unable to interpret it did not bother me," he recalled. In the simple image of repeating dots and bars, he understood that DNA structure had a regular pattern.

Watson was then determined to find work in crystallography. In September 1951, he joined Cambridge's Cavendish Laboratory. Its director was a famed crystallographer, Sir William Lawrence Bragg.

Scientists wondered whether DNA's genetic information could also be in the form of a simple code.

He and his father had shared the 1915 Nobel Prize in Physics for using X-rays to reveal the structure of crystals. But Watson was assigned to study not crystallography but protein, and he soon grew bored.

Watson then met Francis Crick, a 35-year-old graduate student who was his lab mate. Crick was also looking for distraction from his assigned work on protein. Soon they were talking about DNA structure. "Jim and I hit it off immediately," Crick later recalled, "partly because our interests were astonishingly similar and partly, I suspect, because a certain youthful arrogance, a ruthlessness, and an impatience with sloppy thinking came naturally to both of us."

The mop-haired Watson and the lanky Crick discussed ideas over meals and on walks around campus. A brotherly affection grew. Watson, almost 12 years younger than Crick, later said, "I couldn't have got anywhere without Francis. ... It could have been Crick without Watson, but certainly not Watson without Crick."

Meanwhile, the King's College lab seemed poised to discover DNA's structure. Wilkins had been researching DNA for five years by the time Watson and Crick met. In addition, Rosalind Franklin's crystallography techniques were producing some of the best X-ray photographs of DNA in the world.

But Wilkins and Franklin were unable to work together. When Franklin joined King's laboratory in 1951, she believed DNA crystallography research would be hers alone, with help from assistant Raymond Gosling. Meanwhile, Wilkins assumed the highly skilled Franklin was hired to assist him on his own DNA research. Bitterness grew. Wilkins recalled later that he once presented his own X-ray photographs and Franklin told him, "Go back to your microscopes."

At Cambridge, Crick struck upon a strategy.

W.C. Röntgen discovered X-rays in 1895.

PICTURING THE INVISIBLE

By the late 1500s scientists were using microscopes to magnify and see objects not visible with the naked eye. By the late 1600s microscopes were strong enough to reveal a microscopic world that was teeming with bacteria and tiny organisms called protozoa.

But microscopes and visible light were not powerful enough to see chromosomes, which are measured in millionths of a meter. Scientists would need another way to study these tiny objects. The discovery of X-rays allowed scientists to see how molecules and their atoms fit together. X-rays went hand in hand with crystallography. When crystallographers shone X-rays on DNA fibers, the waves bounced and scattered. These diffracted waves created a pattern on a photographic plate. Using elaborate mathematical calculations, scientists could learn the dimensions of an object and could understand its atoms and its three-dimensional structure.

Since W.C. Röntgen won the 1901 Nobel Prize in Physics for discovering X-rays, many more Nobel prizes have been awarded for scientific breakthroughs using X-rays and crystallography. But seeing tiny DNA fibers today is still a challenge, even with sophisticated microscopes and advanced technology.

Unlike Franklin, he admired Linus Pauling's problem-solving methods. "The alpha-helix had not been found by staring at X-ray pictures; the essential trick, instead, was to ask which atoms like to sit next to each other," he later said. "In place of pencil and paper, the main working tools were a set of molecular models superficially resembling the toys of preschool children." As Watson put it, they would "imitate Linus Pauling and beat him at his own game."

But Watson and Crick needed more information to begin building a model. King's laboratory had plenty. They got the first details in November 1951, when Wilkins invited Watson to attend a lecture by Rosalind Franklin. She hinted that chains of chemicals twisting in helices could form the DNA molecule. Afterward, Watson eagerly told Crick about it. But he remembered few details since he had taken no notes.

They plunged into model-building anyway. Watson felt bold. "Too many people want things to be 99 percent proven before they act on it," he said. With much guesswork and Wilkins' idea that DNA contained three sugar-phosphate chains, they quickly constructed a model. Nitrate bases climbed the outside of a triple helix. They invited members of King's laboratory to travel to Cambridge and take a look.

Watson later remembered the visit as "that

"In place of pencil and paper, the main working tools were a set of molecular models superficially resembling the toys of preschool children."

Rosalind Franklin's Photo 51 has been called "the most important photo ever taken."

unfortunate November day." On the other hand, Franklin's assistant, Raymond Gosling, remembered that "it was a happy moment for Rosalind and me because it justified her interpretation that you could build models, but you couldn't prove which was the right one. And here they were, the model builders, hard at it, and they had produced completely the wrong model." Gosling remembered that Franklin "was pretty sharp in her criticism of the model and explained in detail why it couldn't be correct: one, two, three. And then we left."

Bragg was embarrassed by this failure in his lab. He ordered Watson and Crick to leave DNA to the King's scientists. The friends found themselves sidelined in the race. But after Pauling's flawed paper arrived in England a year later, they got a second chance. Bragg realized that his scientists could beat King's, and even Pauling himself. He gave them permission to jump back into the race. Photo 51, which has been called "the most important photo ever taken" by King's College archivist Geoff Browell, would lead the way.

Looking back, Watson concluded that "one reason both of our chief competitors failed to reach the Double Helix before us was that each was effectively very isolated." Pauling, for example, missed the chance to meet with Franklin and see Photo 51 because he was denied permission to travel abroad. After World War II, the U.S. government had anxiously watched the Soviet Union's communist-style government spreading across the world. Because he was an outspoken peace activist, Pauling was falsely accused—along with hundreds of other Americans—of being a communist and enemy of the nation. Pauling would go on to win the Nobel Peace Prize, but that would come years later. In the meantime, he could not work with the British scientists who were studying DNA.

Watson said Franklin's isolated working style prevented King's laboratory from winning the race. He claimed that if she had shared all her evidence with Crick, he "would have told her what it meant. She would have gone back and found the double helix." However, today many people, such as Lynne Osman Elkin, a California State University biology professor, argue that Franklin did not need help—she only needed more time: "She could see things, but unless she could prove them, she wouldn't publish them."

Wilkins felt no pressure to rush his research either. He was waiting until Franklin left for a new job before starting to build a model. On the other hand, Crick and Watson felt great urgency to start building again. Crick asked Wilkins, "Then do you mind if we have a go?" Wilkins reluctantly agreed.

DEPARTMENT OF STATE
WASHINGTON

In reply refer to
F130-Pauling, Linus Carl

FEB 1 4 1952

Dr. Linus Carl Pauling,
    3500 Fairpoint Street,
        Pasadena 8, California.

My dear Dr. Pauling:

In reply to your letter of January 24, 1952, you are informed that your request for a passport has been carefully considered by the Department. However, a passport of this Government is not being issued to you since the Department is of the opinion that your proposed travel would not be in the best interests of the United States.

The passport fee of $9.00 which accompanied the application which you executed on October 17, 1951 will be returned to you at a later date.

Sincerely yours,

R. B. Shipley,
Chief, Passport Division

The U.S. government in 1952 refused to issue a passport to Linus Pauling.

On February 4, 1953, Watson and Crick set to work. Both men had strengths. Crick had a gift for imagining molecular structures without using mathematics. Watson was single-minded about their goal. He once said that "in the game of science—or life—the highest goal isn't simply to win, it's to win at something really difficult."

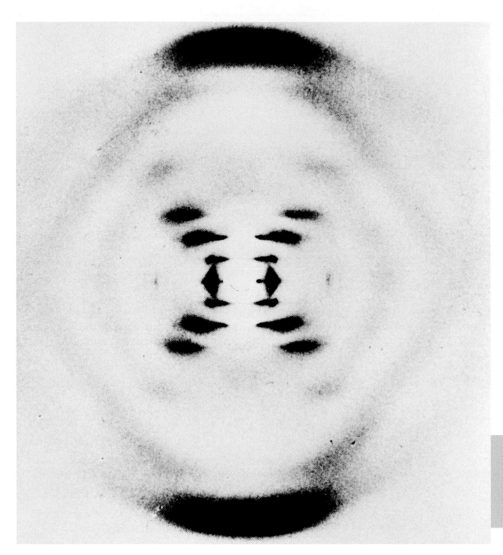

Photo 51 did not reveal that DNA was a double helix. But Franklin's notes did. The pair were lucky to come across Franklin's data once again—and used it without her knowledge. A fellow scientist at the Cavendish Laboratory passed along a copy of a 1952 report on DNA research by King's laboratory. It included Franklin's latest findings, which had not yet been published. Watson later admitted that Franklin "of course, did not directly give us her data. For that

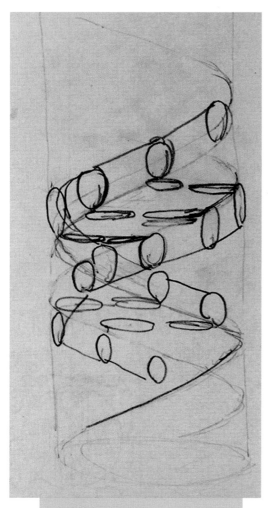

Francis Crick sketched the structure of DNA in 1953.

matter, no one at King's realized [the information was] in our hands."

Franklin had determined that DNA's structure was simple—and symmetrical. Crick knew the symmetry confirmed that DNA was composed of two chains twisting in opposite directions, a double helix. Watson pointed out that in nature "important biological objects come in pairs."

But did the bases fit inside the chains or on the outside? Watson was still unsure as he worked with the cardboard pieces and rods. Yet again, Franklin's 1952 report offered the answer. Franklin concluded that the chains formed a frame to contain the bases inside. They even borrowed her measurements to build two accurately spaced chains of phosphates.

The double helix model was taking shape at the Cavendish Laboratory. But Crick and Watson were stumped by one last problem. How did the nitrogen bases fit inside the chains to form the rungs of the ladder structure? They tried matching similar bases to each other. But adenine and guanine nucleotides are larger molecules than cytosine and thymine. This arrangement created an awkward model with rungs of different lengths and sizes. Crick insisted that Chargaff's discovery—that the amounts of adenine and thymine were almost the same as were the amounts of cytosine and guanine—was an important clue.

On the morning of February 28, 1953, Watson was struck by a brilliant and original idea. Looking at the model pieces, he suddenly realized that if he joined adenine and thymine, the pair was the same shape as a guanine and cytosine pair. Watson joined the two nucleotide pairs and fit them neatly inside the double chains. Chargaff's ratio now made perfect sense.

When Crick saw the elegant model, he knew it was right. The structure held the answer to how DNA can reproduce to fill countless cells with identical genetic information. The chains spiraling toward each other unzip to form two separate strands. Each strand serves as a template for a new strand to form. More nucleotides slide in to match up with their companion nucleotides—adenine with thymine and guanine with cytosine—to construct an exact copy of the original double helix.

Crick and Watson headed triumphantly to The Eagle, their usual nearby lunch spot. Beneath a ceiling covered by graffiti left by World War II airmen, the British and American scientists took a back table. Crick could not contain his excitement. Watson recalled that his partner told "everyone within hearing distance that we had found the secret of life."

By March 7, a finished model made of newly cut and polished metal pieces was ready to show visitors. Wilkins was awestruck by the model, which he said

Crick (left) and Watson at the Cavendish Lab in Cambridge

had "a life of its own" and "seemed to speak for itself, saying—'I don't care what you think—I know I am right.'"

Visitors were also struck by the simplicity of the solution: "The whole business was like a child's toy that you could buy at the dime store," said biophysicist Max Delbrück, "all built in this wonderful way that you could explain in *Life* magazine so that really a five-year-old can understand what's going on. This was the greatest surprise for everyone."

But some visitors had mixed feelings. "That we had found the double helix without doing experiments irked them," Watson said. Most scientists would need to see more than a graceful model to believe in the discovery. When Franklin visited, she remarked, "It's very pretty, but how are they going to prove it?" They would need her help one last time.

On April 25, 1953, *Nature* magazine published three articles about the discovery. Watson and Crick flipped a coin to determine the order of their names to be listed with the article. Franklin and Wilkins each wrote an article presenting X-ray evidence and data to support Watson and Crick's model.

In 1962 Watson, Crick, and Wilkins shared the Nobel Prize in Physiology or Medicine. It was given "for their discoveries concerning the molecular structure of nucleic acids and its significance for information transfer in living material." Franklin had died four years earlier and could not be included since winners must be living. But the winners' speeches did not even mention her.

"That we had found the double helix without doing experiments irked them."

Nobel Prize winners in 1962 included (from left) Maurice Wilkins, Max Perutz, Francis Crick, John Steinbeck, James Watson, and John Kendrew.

"The major credit I think Jim and I deserve," said Crick decades later, "is for selecting the right problem and sticking to it." He also admitted that the path to success had been lined with both good fortune and mistakes. "It's true that by blundering about we stumbled on gold," he wrote, "but the fact remains that we were looking for gold. Both of us had decided, quite independently of each other, that the central problem in molecular biology was the chemical structure of the gene."

ChapterFour
NEW QUESTIONS

With a magician's flair, Linus Pauling pulled aside a curtain at the end of a lecture in 1951. There stood his elegantly twisting model of the alpha helix, and an audience applauded. James Watson and Francis Crick raced to solve DNA's structure and to also reveal it dramatically. Otherwise, Crick said, it "would have trickled out and … its impact would have been far less." Sixty years after the 1953 publication of the papers on DNA structure, Adam Rutherford, a former editor of the journal *Nature*, called it "a turning point: our understanding of life was changed forever that day, and the modern era of biology began."

Like magicians, Watson and Crick solved the DNA structure, but they also pulled aside a curtain on a new problem. Scientists understood how DNA looked, but now they wanted to know how it worked. Six feet (1.8 m) of DNA are locked inside each cell nucleus, coiled into chromosomes. How can the DNA's genes send protein-making instructions to the cell's cytoplasm? Proteins keep the body alive. They make up blood, bone, muscle, and brain cells. They allow humans to move, digest food, grow, think, and survive. In short, as explained by the Pulitzer Prize-winning science writer Siddhartha Mukherjee, proteins have the job of "bringing genes to life."

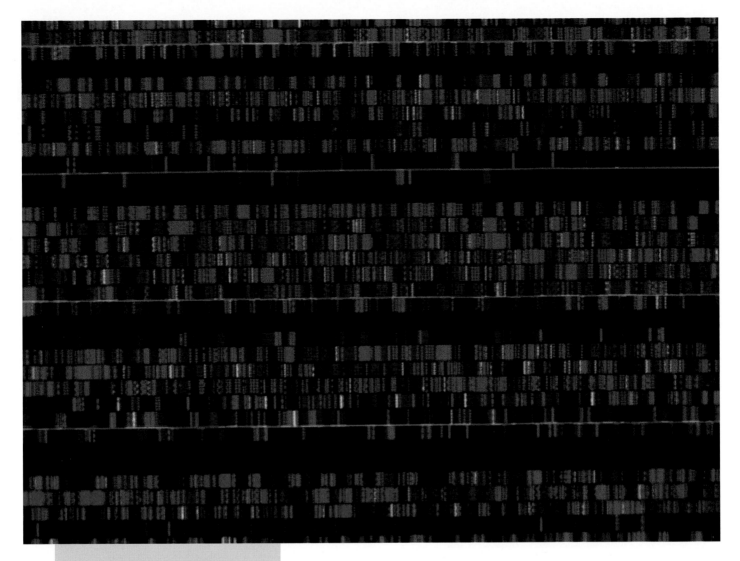

A computer screen displays a human DNA sequence as a series of colored bands. DNA consists of two long strands linked by the interactions of bases. Each color represents a specific base.

Watson and other scientists in 1954 formed an informal club that was dedicated to understanding how cells make proteins. Crick, Chargaff, Sydney Brenner, and others wore neckties embroidered with a yellow helix—but not the double helix. It was a single twisting strand of DNA's nucleic acid partner, ribonucleic acid. They knew RNA was involved in making protein, but they did not yet understand that DNA's genetic message was useless without RNA.

Once the DNA puzzle was solved, Francis Crick and others turned to the role of RNA.

Crick gave an unforgettable lecture in 1957 that changed the way biologists thought about life. He argued that the main job of genes was to make proteins. "Once the central and unique role of proteins is admitted," said Crick, "there seems little point in genes' doing anything else." Over lunch one day in April 1960, Crick, Brenner, and French scientist François Jacob realized that a "messenger molecule" must carry DNA's genetic message out of

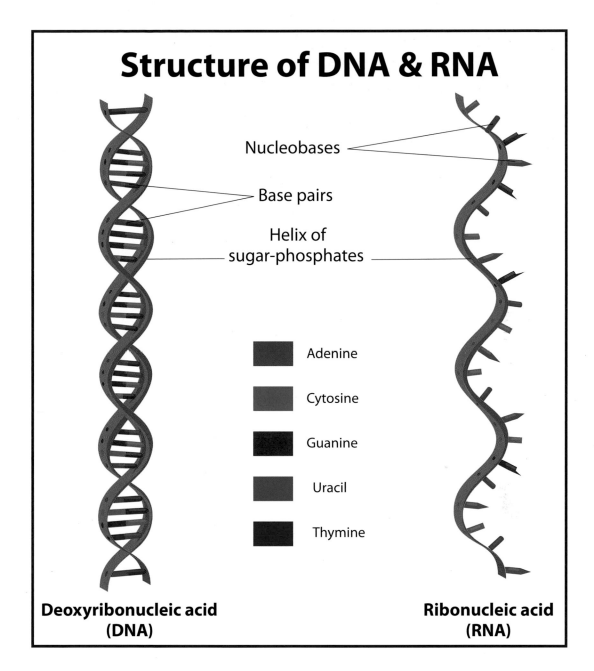

Structure of DNA & RNA

Nucleobases

Base pairs

Helix of
sugar-phosphates

Adenine

Cytosine

Guanine

Uracil

Thymine

**Deoxyribonucleic acid
(DNA)**

**Ribonucleic acid
(RNA)**

the nucleus. They wondered whether it was a protein or a nucleic acid.

Crick and Brenner guessed that the messenger was RNA, and they were right. RNA helps DNA make proteins. DNA unzips and a strand of RNA forms along the nucleotides, copying the order of the nucleotides. RNA records DNA's message with the same alphabet of nucleotides. But RNA's alphabet uses uracil instead of thymine.

At this stage, messenger RNA exits the nucleus and carries its message to ribosomes in the cytoplasm, the jellylike substance that fills a cell. Ribosomes are factories that scan RNA's sequence of nucleotides. The RNA instructs the ribosomes to string together amino acids. These building blocks of proteins are called polypeptides. RNA makes it possible for DNA's nucleotides to be translated into the proteins necessary for life.

A new race was on. Watson and Crick had predicted in 1953 that the sequence of nucleotides "is the code which carries the genetic information." Now scientists wanted to learn to read DNA's message. Like wartime code breakers, scientists went to work on DNA's alphabet of nucleotides. Crick helped discover that DNA is in fact a triple-letter code. The three nucleotides in each set, called a codon, work together like letters in a word. Each codon matches one of 20 amino acids. These amino acids form long chains, like sentences. These polypeptides form the many proteins needed by organisms.

In 1961 a 34-year-old American biochemist deciphered the first codon in the genetic code. Crick was at a biochemistry conference in Moscow where Marshall Nirenberg announced the discovery. By

Marshall Nirenberg
experimented with DNA
to help decipher the
genetic code.

1966 scientists had matched nearly all 64 possible
codons to their amino acids. With the help of Crick
and Brenner, all 64 codons were identified by 1967.

Scientists rushed onward to the next new question. In his 1962 Nobel Prize lecture, Crick had wondered aloud: "Is the code universal, that is, the same in all organisms?" He answered: "Preliminary evidence suggests that it may well be." Evidence soon confirmed that DNA, RNA, amino acids, and proteins seemed to be the language of all living organisms.

In the 1970s scientists began the laborious process of studying the order of DNA nucleotides in many organisms. The process is called sequencing the genome. They found that particular combinations of nucleotides—not the number of nucleotides—are what make life forms unique. For example, 2 billion base pairs can be arranged to create a boa constrictor or a bat. About 3 billion base pairs can be arranged to create a human or a pig. Scientists had finally learned the basics of DNA language. With this hard-won knowledge, scientists were now ready for a daring next step.

Two decades after Watson and Crick discussed DNA over gooseberry pie at The Eagle, two other scientists did the same over corned beef sandwiches in a deli in the Waikiki neighborhood of Honolulu, Hawaii. American biochemists Herbert Boyer and Stanley Cohen would start a revolution in biology. They would rewrite DNA's code.

In 1973 they used an enzyme to cut apart bacteria's DNA. Next they inserted genes from a toad

Herbert Boyer stood in front of a projection of DNA structure at the University of California Medical Center.

into bacteria's DNA. Boyer recalls the "moment I'll never forget." The bacteria not only multiplied with the new DNA sequence inside, but they also produced toad protein. It was clear that DNA was a universal language, understood across all species. "One of the things that was so revolutionary, I guess, about this technology was that it was so easy," Boyer said.

Business people quickly recognized a moneymaking opportunity. American biochemist Paul Berg remembered that "companies sprung up almost like mushrooms, you know, after a rain." Investors took a new interest in biologists who could alter DNA—those who could genetically engineer products necessary to daily life. Biotechnology companies competed to produce better medicine and food more quickly and cheaply. The reward was not simply the satisfaction of winning a race. Biotech companies can be worth hundreds of billions of dollars.

The first genetically engineered food to be sold, a new kind of tomato, appeared in grocery stores in 1994. The tomatoes stayed firm longer than the normal variety because scientists had deactivated the gene in them that causes fruit to soften. Scientists continue to adjust genes in crops to better resist pests, survive drought, and produce more food. Today almost all corn and soybeans grown in the U.S. are genetically engineered.

Knowledge about DNA also saves lives. Human DNA inserted into bacterial DNA helps create life-saving substances that human bodies cannot produce, such as insulin for diabetics and a blood-clotting protein for hemophiliacs. This technology might someday avert a pandemic, according to the U.S. Food and Drug Administration. Each year drug companies scramble to produce

A scientist drilled holes in eggs, which were then injected with flu viruses. It is part of a study to produce successful flu vaccines.

vaccines to lessen the symptoms of the latest flu strain. Using genetically programmed insect cells, vaccines can be produced faster and distributed sooner than ever.

Genetics also helps to make the environment cleaner. Scientists mapped the genome of oil-eating bacteria to identify useful genes for cleaning up oil spills in the ocean. They are also genetically engineering bacteria from human intestines to produce fuel that does not pollute the air.

Despite its benefits, some people have found genetic engineering alarming since the earliest experiments. Concerned scientists gathered in California in 1975 to discuss how to conduct genetic research without causing harm. The federal government later established a committee to monitor research on genetically engineered nucleic molecules.

People are still concerned that genetic engineering is dangerous. They worry that genetically engineered food will cause unknown damage to people and animals. They worry about medical experiments that alter DNA by deactivating genes or adding new ones to cure diseases. For example, Chinese scientists recently tried—unsuccessfully—to genetically engineer nonviable human embryos, which cannot result in a birth. They hoped to remove disease-causing genes.

Some scientists themselves worry. Geneticist Eric Schadt argues, "We don't really understand enough of the genome to be making these types of changes." Another geneticist, who did not want to be identified in a newspaper interview, wondered whether scientists will take their knowledge of DNA too far. "You can argue that it could be hugely beneficial to correct genetic diseases, but on the other hand we don't know

MAPS INSTEAD OF MODELS

A scientist used a sequencing machine in his work on the Human Genome Project.

Alfred Sturtevant mapped the locations of fruit fly genes on a chromosome in 1913. In the 1970s scientists examined a bacterium's 5,375 nucleotides to map the first genome of a living organism. Years later scientists raced to tackle the human genome, with its 6 billion nucleotides bundled inside 20,500 genes.

James Watson worried that biotech businesses would win this race. He helped persuade the U.S. government to spend more money on studying the human genome. For more than a decade, thousands of scientists worked on the Human Genome Project. They cut the DNA into short sections and sorted them with computers.

The government-funded program cooperated with a private genomics company to complete the map in 2003. They had discovered that all humans share 99.9 percent of the same genetic information.

But the 0.1 percent of difference in people's genes makes them as distinct as their fingerprints. A lab can use DNA from a single hair taken from a crime scene to determine whether it belongs to a suspect. Scientists can sample DNA in 13,000-year-old bones to learn about human ancestors.

Mapping the genome can provide insight into a person's health. "Sequencing a gene is like reading a book one letter at a time to look for any spelling mistakes," explained a physician in a Boston hospital's genetics diagnostic lab. Some "spelling mistakes" cause disease, while others do not. Diseases can result from an error in just one letter of the genetic code.

Mapping human genes now is faster and less expensive than ever. It took 13 years and cost $3 billion to complete the first human genome in 2003. Today it takes hours and costs less than $1,000.

it's safe and it's a slippery slope. How long will it be before people try to alter eye and hair color, and height and intelligence?" he asked.

But experimentation with DNA's possibilities probably cannot be stopped. Human Genome Project director Francis Collins said Watson and Crick's discovery of DNA's structure "is so intertwined in every bit of what we do experimentally, in terms of perceiving our own position in the scheme of life on this planet. It has become one of those givens that is so central to your thinking that you stop thinking about it, but if somebody took it away from you, your whole intellectual foundation would collapse, and it would be unimaginable what we would be doing now if we didn't know about the double helix."

Scientists have even gone beyond working with existing DNA to create an artificial version of it. In 2016 they constructed an entire simple cell genome using synthetic DNA that had been made in a lab.

Despite the power of scientists to cut, mix, and create DNA, the double helix remains largely a mystery. Learning how it creates life is not easy. Scientists still do not understand the function of almost a third of genes found on chromosomes. For Scottish bioengineer Alistair Elfick, this is good news: "Finding so many genes without a known function is unsettling, but it's exciting because it's left us with much still to learn."

"Finding so many genes without a known function is unsettling, but it's exciting because it's left us with much still to learn."

The mysterious double helix still holds many secrets.

Timeline

1859

Charles Darwin explains the concept of natural selection and introduces his theory of evolution

1866

Gregor Mendel publishes his data from pea experiments, which prove the laws of heredity

1869

Swiss biologist Friedrich Miescher isolates DNA

1910

American biologist Thomas Morgan confirms Mendel's findings in experiments with fruit flies and discovers that genes are located on chromosomes

1913

American geneticist Alfred H. Sturtevant makes the first gene map

1900

English biologist William Bateson comes across Mendel's work and promotes it around the world

1903

German biologist Theodor Boveri and American geneticist Walter Sutton conclude that chromosomes contain all hereditary information necessary for an organism to grow and function

1944

Canadian-born researcher Oswald Avery discovers that genes are made of DNA

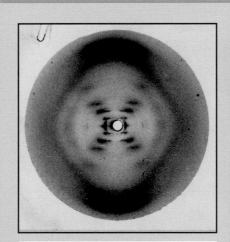

1952

English biophysicist Rosalind Franklin takes Photo 51 using a crystallography technique

1953

American biologist James Watson and English biophysicist Francis Crick, with contributions from Franklin and Maurice Wilkins, discover the double helix structure of DNA

Timeline

1957

Crick argues that the main function of genes is to make proteins

1961

American biochemist Marshall Nirenberg and a colleague decipher the first codon of the genetic code

1962

Watson, Crick, and Maurice Wilkins receive the Nobel Prize in Physiology or Medicine

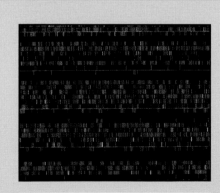

2003

Human genome map is complete

2010

Neanderthal genome yields insights into human evolution

1967

All 64 codons are identified and the genetic code is cracked

1973

First organisms (bacteria) are genetically engineered by American biochemists Herbert Boyer and Stanley Cohen

1994

First genetically engineered food appears in markets

2013

700,000-year-old horse genome shatters the age record for ancient DNA

2017

Food and Drug Administration proposes regulations to deal with edited DNA

Glossary

amino acids—small molecules that form into chains that fold into various shapes to make proteins

codon—series of three nucleotides in a row that carries genetic code for a specific amino acid

double helix—spiral arrangement of the two complementary strands of DNA

enzyme—kind of protein that creates chemical reactions in living organisms

gene—unit of DNA located on a chromosome that carries information about one or more traits and is the basic unit by which genetic information is passed from parent to offspring

genome—an organism's complete set of DNA, including all of its genes

heredity—genetic characteristics as passed down by an organism's ancestors

molecule—atoms connected by chemical bonds that form the smallest unit of a substance

nucleotide—any of a group of molecules that, when linked, form the building blocks of DNA or RNA

nonviable—not able to develop, grow, or survive

nucleus—part of the cell that controls all activities in the cell and contains genetic information

polypeptide—chain of amino acids that is part of a protein molecule

ribosomes—protein builders of a cell

template—nucleic acid molecule that acts as a pattern for the sequence of assembly of a protein, nucleic acid, or other large molecule

Additional Resources

Further Reading

Albright, R.N. *The Double Helix Structure of DNA: James Watson, Francis Crick, Maurice Wilkins, and Rosalind Franklin.*
New York: Rosen Publishing Group, 2014.

Mooney, Carla. *Genetics: Breaking the Code of Your DNA.* White River Junction, Vt.: Nomad Press, 2014.

Rooney, Anne. *Genetic Engineering and Developments in Biotechnology.*
New York: Crabtree Publishing Company, 2017.

Swaby, Rachel. *Headstrong: 52 Women Who Changed Science—and the World.*
New York: Broadway Books, 2015.

Internet Sites

Use FactHound to find Internet sites related to this book.
Visit *www.facthound.com*
Just type in 9780756556426 and go.

Critical Thinking Questions

James Watson said the double helix was going to be found soon, possibly in a year or two, if he and Francis Crick had not found it in 1953. Who do you think could have found it and why? Why do you think it was Watson and Crick who presented an accurate model to the world first? Use evidence from the text to support your answer.

Genetic engineering in agriculture and medicine has inspired much debate. Do you think it is helpful? Do you consider it too risky to use?

In 1944 Erwin Schrödinger wondered *What Is Life?* in his book by that title. Nine years later Watson claimed that he and Crick had discovered the answer, the "secret of life." What do you think Watson meant by this phrase? In the decades since, how have other scientists helped to answer Schrödinger's question?

Source Notes

Page 4, line 18: Arthur W. Wiggins and Charles M. Wynn Sr. *The Human Side of Science: Edison and Tesla, Watson and Crick, and Other Personal Stories Behind Science's Big Ideas.* Amherst, N.Y.: Prometheus Books, 2016, p. 239.

Page 7, line 7: James D. Watson. *The Double Helix: A Personal Account of the Discovery of the Structure of DNA.* New York: W.W. Norton & Company, 1980, p. 25.

Page 10, line 2: Jim Holt. "Photo Finish: Rosalind Franklin and the great DNA Race." *The New Yorker.* 28 Oct. 2002. 1 Feb. 2017. http://www.newyorker.com/magazine/2002/10/28/photo-finish-2

Page 10, line 21: "Celebrating Rosalind Franklin: a perfect example of single-minded devotion to research." Grrlscientist. *The Guardian.* 25 July 2013. 21 April 2017. https://www.theguardian.com/science/grrlscientist/2013/jul/25/rosalind-franklin-google-doodle-science-dna-viruses

Page 10, line 27: Siddhartha Mukherjee. *The Gene: An Intimate History.* New York: Scribner, 2016, p. 154

Page 11, line 1: Ibid.

Page 12, line 4: Ibid., p. 156.

Page 12, line 9: *The Double Helix: A Personal Account of the Discovery of the Structure of DNA,* p. 99

Page 13, col. 1, line 9: "Secret of Photo 51." *Nova.* PBS. 22 April 2003. 2 Feb. 2017. http://www.pbs.org/wgbh/nova/transcripts/3009_photo51.html

Page 13, col. 1, line 18: "Rosalind Franklin's Legacy." *Nova.* PBS. 22 April 2003. 1 Feb. 2017. http://www.pbs.org/wgbh/nova/tech/rosalind-franklin-legacy.html

Page 13, col. 1, line 23: Natalie Starkey. "Would Rosalind Franklin have won a Nobel for her work on viruses?" *The Guardian.* 25 July 2013. 21 April 2017. https://www.theguardian.com/science/blog/2013/jul/25/rosalind-franklin-nobel-viruses-google-doodle

Page 13, col. 1, line 25: "Watson and Crick describe structure of DNA 1953." *A Science Odyssey.* PBS. 21 April 2017. http://www.pbs.org/wgbh/aso/databank/entries/do53dn.html

Page 13, col. 2, line 9: Lynn Elkin. "Rosalind Elsie Franklin 1920–1958." Jewish Women's Archive. 21 April 2017. https://jwa.org/encyclopedia/article/franklin-rosalind

Page 14, line 2: James D. Watson. *DNA: The Secret of Life.* New York: Alfred A Knopf, 2003, p. 53.

Page 14, line 11: James D. Watson. *The Annotated and Illustrated Double Helix.* New York: Simon and Schuster, 2012, p. 212.

Page 14, line 19: "Double Helix Double Cross? A Survey of Recent Articles." *The Wilson Quarterly.* Summer 2003. 21 April 2017. http://archive.wilsonquarterly.com/in-essence/double-helix-double-cross-survey-recent-articles

Page 20, line 6: *The Gene: An Intimate History,* p. 62.

Page 22, line 9: Ibid., p. 111.

Page 23, line 15: Nathaniel Comfort. "Genes Are Overrated." *The Atlantic.* June 2016. 21 April 2017. http://www.theatlantic.com/magazine/archive/2016/06/genes-are-overrated/480729/

Page 24, col. 1, line 1: Matthew Cobb. "Oswald T Avery, the unsung hero of genetic science." *The Guardian.* 3 June 2013. 21 April 2017. https://theguardian.com/science/blog/2013/jun/03/oswald-t-avery-genetic-science-dna

Page 24, col. 2, line 13: The Oswald T. Avery Collection. U.S. National Library of Medicine. National Institutes of Health. 21 April 2017. https://profiles.nlm.nih.gov/CC/

Page 25, line 21: Leslie A. Pray, PhD. "Discovery of DNA structure and function: Watson and Crick." *Nature Education.* 2008. 21 April 2017. http://www.nature.com/scitable/topicpage/discovery-of-dna-structure-and-function-watson-397

Page 26, line 1: "Obituary: Francis Crick." 29 July 2004. 24 April 2017. BBC News. http://news.bbc.co.uk/2/hi/science/nature/2551009.stm

Page 26, line 11: Erwin Schrödinger. *What Is Life?* 1944. 24 April 2017. http://www.whatislife.ie/downloads/What-is-Life.pdf

Page 26, line 13: James Watson. "Succeeding in Science: Some Rules of Thumb." *Science.* September 1993. Linus Pauling and the Race for DNA. Special Collections and Archives Research Center, Oregon State University Libraries. 24 April 2017. http://scarc.library.oregonstate.edu/coll/pauling/dna/quotes/all.html

Page 28, line 20: *The Gene: An Intimate History,* p. 46.

Page 29, line 9: *What Mad Pursuit: A Personal View of Scientific Discovery,* p. 64

Page 30, line 8: "Key Participants. James D. Watson." Linus Pauling and the Race for DNA. Special Collections and Archives Research Center, Oregon State University Libraries. 24 April 2017. http://scarc.library.oregonstate.edu/coll/pauling/dna/people/watson.html

Page 30, line 26: Matt Ridley. *Francis Crick: Discoverer of the Genetic Code.* New York: Atlas Books, 2006, p. 51.

Page 32, line 2: *The Gene: An Intimate History,* p. 148.

Page 32, line 8: "Watson and Crick." Linus Pauling and the Race for DNA. Special Collections and Archives Research Center, Oregon State University Libraries. http://scarc.library.oregonstate.edu/coll/pauling/dna/narrative/page8.html

Page 32, line 20: *Francis Crick: Discoverer of the Genetic Code,* p. 48.

Page 32, line 28: James D. Watson. *DNA: The Secret of Life.* New York: Alfred A. Knopf, 2003, p. 48.

Page 33, line 3: "Secret of Photo 51."

Page 33, line 9: Ibid.

Page 33, line 20: Fergus Walsh. "The most important photo every taken?" BBC News. 16 May 2012. 24 April 2017. http://www.bbc.com/news/health-18041884

Page 33, line 23: "Succeeding in Science: Some Rules of Thumb."

Page 34, line 15: David Ewing Duncan. Discover Dialogue: Geneticist James Watson. *Discover.* 1 July 2003. 24 April 2017. http://discovermagazine.com/2003/jul/featdialogue

Page 34, line 21: "Rosalind Franklin's Legacy."

Page 34, line 27: *Francis Crick: Discoverer of the Genetic Code,* p. 66.

Page 35, line 5: "Quotes by or related to James Watson." Linus Pauling and the Race for DNA. Special Collections and Archives Research Center, Oregon State University Libraries. 24 April 2017. http://scarc.library.oregonstate.edu/coll/pauling/dna/quotes/james_watson.html

Page 36, line 9: James D. Watson. *The Double Helix: A Personal Account of the Discovery of the Structure of DNA.* Nature Publishing Group. 1953. University of Washington. 24 April 2017. http://faculty.washington.edu/hqian/amath532/Watson_The_Double_Helix.pdf

Page 37, line 7: *The Gene: An Intimate History,* p. 154.

Page 38, line 23: *The Double Helix: A Personal Account of the Discovery of the Structure of DNA,* p. 115.

Page 39, line 1: *The Gene: An Intimate History,* p. 158

Page 40, line 2: "Quotes." Max Delbruck. *The Eighth Day of Creation.* 1979. Linus Pauling and the Race for DNA. Special Collections and Archives Research Center, Oregon State University Libraries. 24 April 2017. http://scarc.library.oregonstate.edu/coll/pauling/dna/quotes/all.html

Page 40, line 8: *DNA: The Secret of Life,* p. 55.

Page 40, line 12: Jim Holt. "Photo Finish: Rosalind Franklin and the great DNA race." *The New Yorker.* 28 Oct. 2002. 24 April 2017. http://www.newyorker.com/magazine/2002/10/28/photo-finish-2

Page 40, line 23: The Nobel Prize in Physiology or Medicine 1962. 24 April 2017. https://www.nobelprize.org/nobel_prizes/medicine/laureates/1962/

Page 41, line 1: *What Mad Pursuit: A Personal View of Scientific Discovery,* p. 74.

Page 41, line 5: Nicholas Wade. "Crick, Who Discovered DNA Structure With Watson, Dies." *The New York Times.* 29 July 2004. 24 April 2017. http://www.nytimes.com/2004/07/29/science/crick-who-discovered-dna-structure-with-watson-dies.html?_r=0

Page 42, line 6: *What Mad Pursuit: A Personal View of Scientific Discovery,* p. 76.

Page 42, line 10: Adam Rutherford. "DNA double helix: discovery that led to 60 years of biological revolution." *The Guardian.* 25 April 2013. 24 April 2017. https://www.theguardian.com/science/2013/apr/25/dna-double-helix-60-years-biological-revolution

Page 42, line 25: *The Gene: An Intimate History,* p. 169

Page 44, line 4: Genetics and Genomics Timeline 1957. Genome News Network. 24 April 2017. http://www.genomenewsnetwork.org/resources/timeline/1957_Crick.php

Page 46, line 14: Sahotra Sarkar. *The Philosphy and History of Molecular Biology: New Perspectives.* Boston: Kluwer Academic Publishers, 1996, p. 191.

Page 48, line 3: Nobel Lecture: On the Genetic Code. 11 Dec. 1962, 24 April 2017. http://www.nobelprize.org/nobel_prizes/medicine/laureates/1962/crick-lecture.html

Page 49, line 1: "DNA. Playing God." PBS. 21 March 2013. 24 April 2017. https://www.youtube.com/watch?v=M3wg-W3Slow

Page 49, line 6: Ibid

Page 50, line 3: Interview transcript: Paul Berg. 8 Dec. 2001. 24 April 2017. https://www.nobelprize.org/nobel_prizes/chemistry/laureates/1980/berg-interview-transcript.html

Page 52, line 22: Ashley Welch. "Designer baby controversy: Scientists edit genome of human embryo." CBS News. 24 April 2015. 24 April 2017. http://www.cbsnews.com/news/designer-baby-controversy-scientists-edit-genome-of-human-embryo/

Page 52, line 26: Ian Sample. "Scientists genetically modify human embryos in controversial world first." *The Guardian.* 23 April 2015. 24 April 2017. https://www.theguardian.com/science/2015/apr/23/scientists-genetically-modify-human-embryos-in-controversial-world-first

Page 53, col. 2, line 8: Bonnie Rochman. "Time Explains: Genome Sequencing. *Time.* 22 Oct. 2012. 24 April 2017. http://healthland.time.com/2012/10/22/time-explains-genome-sequencing/

Page 54, line 7: "The DNA Revolution." NPR. 24 April 2017. http://www.npr.org/news/specials/dnaanniversary/

Page 54, line 26: Andy Coghlan. "Artificial cell designed in lab reveals genes essential to life." *New Scientist.* 24 March 2016. 24 April 2017. https://www.newscientist.com/article/2082278-artificial-cell-designed-in-lab-reveals-genes-essential-to-life/

Select Bibliography

Cobb, Matthew. "Oswald T Avery, the unsung hero of genetic science." *The Guardian*. 3 June 2013. 21 April 2017. https://www.theguardian.com/science/blog/2013/jun/03/oswald-t-avery-genetic-science-dna

Comfort, Nathaniel. "Genes Are Overrated." *The Atlantic*. June 2016. 21 April 2017. http://www.theatlantic.com/magazine/archive/2016/06/genes-are-overrated/480729/

Crick, Francis. *What Mad Pursuit: A Personal View Of Scientific Discovery*. New York: Basic Books, 1988.

DNA From the Beginning. Cold Spring Harbor Laboratory. 25 April 2017. http://www.dnaftb.org

"The DNA Revolution." NPR. 24 April 2017. http://www.npr.org/news/specials/dnaanniversary/

"Double Helix Double Cross? A Survey of Recent Articles." *The Wilson Quarterly*. Summer 2003. 21 April 2017. http://archive.wilsonquarterly.com/in-essence/double-helix-double-cross-survey-recent-articles

Duncan, David Ewing. Discover Dialogue: Geneticist James Watson. *Discover*. 1 July 2003. 24 April 2017. http://discovermagazine.com/2003/jul/featdialogue

Elkin, Lynn. "Rosalind Elsie Franklin 1920–1958." Jewish Women's Archive. 21 April 2017. https://jwa.org/encyclopedia/article/franklin-rosalind

Holt, Jim. "Photo Finish: Rosalind Franklin and the great DNA race." *The New Yorker*. 28 Oct. 2002. 1 Feb. 2017. http://www.newyorker.com/magazine/2002/10/28/photo-finish-2

Linus Pauling and the Race for DNA. Special Collections and Archives Research Center, Oregon State University Libraries. 24 April 2017. http://scarc.library.oregonstate.edu/coll/pauling/dna/index.html

Mukherjee, Siddhartha. *The Gene: An Intimate History*. New York: Scribner, 2016.

The Nobel Prize in Physiology or Medicine 1962. 24 April 2017. https://www.nobelprize.org/nobel_prizes/medicine/laureates/1962/

The Oswald T. Avery Collection. U.S. National Library of Medicine. National Institutes of Health. 21 April 2017. https://profiles.nlm.nih.gov/CC/

An Overview of the Human Genome Project. National Human Genome Research Institute. 25 April 2017. https://www.genome.gov/12011238/an-overview-of-the-human-genome-project/

Pray, Leslie A. "Discovery of DNA structure and function: Watson and Crick." *Nature Education*. 2008. 21 April 2017. http://www.nature.com/scitable/topicpage/discovery-of-dna-structure-and-function-watson-397

Ridley, Matt. *Francis Crick: Discoverer of the Genetic Code*. New York: Atlas Books, 2006.

Rochman, Bonnie. "Time Explains: Genome Sequencing. *Time*. 22 Oct. 2012. 24 April 2017. http://healthland.time.com/2012/10/22/time-explains-genome-sequencing/

Rutherford, Adam. "DNA double helix: discovery that led to 60 years of biological revolution." *The Guardian*. 25 April 2013. 24 April 2017. https://www.theguardian.com/science/2013/apr/25/dna-double-helix-60-years-biological-revolution

Schrödinger, Erwin. *What Is Life?* Cambridge, England: The University Press, 1944.

"Secret of Photo 51." Nova. Transcripts. PBS. 22 April 2003. 2 Feb. 2017. http://www.pbs.org/wgbh/nova/transcripts/3009_photo51.html

Starkey, Natalie. "Would Rosalind Franklin have won a Nobel for her work on viruses?" *The Guardian*. 25 July 2013. 21 April 2017. https://www.theguardian.com/science/blog/2013/jul/25/rosalind-franklin-nobel-viruses-google-doodle

U.S. National Library of Medicine. National Institutes of Health. 25 April 2017. http://www.ncbi.nlm.nih.gov/pmc/articles/

Walsh, Fergus. "The most important photo every taken?" BBC News. 16 May 2012. 24 April 2017. http://www.bbc.com/news/health-18041884

"Watson and Crick describe structure of DNA 1953." *A Science Odyssey*. PBS. 21 April 2017. http://www.pbs.org/wgbh/aso/databank/entries/do53dn.html

Watson, James D. *The Annotated and Illustrated Double Helix*. New York: Simon and Schuster, 2012.

Watson, James D. *Avoid Boring People: Lessons from a Life in Science*. New York: Oxford University Press, 2007.

Watson, James D. *DNA: The Secret of Life*. New York: Alfred A. Knopf, 2003.

James D. Watson. *The Double Helix: A Personal Account of the Discovery of the Structure of DNA*. New York: W.W. Norton & Company, 1980.

Wiggins, Arthur W., and Charles M. Wynn Sr. *The Human Side of Science: Edison and Tesla, Watson and Crick, and Other Personal Stories Behind Science's Big Ideas*. Amherst, N.Y.: Prometheus Books, 2016.

Index

About the Author

As a former teacher, Danielle Smith-Llera taught children to think and write about literature before writing books for them herself. As the spouse of a diplomat, she enjoys living in both Washington, D.C., and overseas in countries such as India, Jamaica, and Romania.